# BONE ANTLER STONE

*Poems*

Tim Miller

✣S4N BOOKS

1. Chauvet Cave
2. Lascaux Cave
3. Altamira Cave
4. The Village of Dolní Vestonice
5. The Village of Gönnersdorf
6. Star Carr
7. Newgrange
8. The Seeress of Vix
9. The Bath Hot Springs
10. Navan Fort
11. Goat's Hole Cave (Red Lady of Paviland)
12. Oleneostrovskii Mogilinik Cemetery
13. Skateholm Cemetery
14. Aerø Boat Burial
15. Isle of Gotland (Ajvide Girl)
16. Stonehenge (Amesbury Archer)
17. Tormarton Ditch
18. Jutland (Egtved Girl)
19. Magdalenenberg Burial Mound
20. Clemency Burial Mound
21. Haraldskaer Woman (Denmark)
   Tollund Man
   Grauballe Man
22. Kayhausen Boy
23. Damendorf Man
24. Lindow Man
25. Lespugue (Female Figurines)
26. Laussel (Female Figurines)
27. Hohle Fels (Female Figurines)
28. Willendorf (Female Figurines)
29. Brassempouy (Female Figurines)
30. Rathlin Island (Axes)
31. Nebra
32. Uluburun Shipwreck
33. Flag Fen (Bronze Offerings in the Water)
34. Battersea
35. Clermont-Ferrand

Praise for ***Bone Antler Stone:***

"Our prehistory now has its poet laureate. Tim Miller makes old stones and artefacts sing with new life."
> – Barry Cunliffe, Emeritus Professor of European Archaeology,
> University of Oxford

"The scope of this collection is extraordinary, and the depth of research admirable. But Tim Miller's poetry wears its learning well enough to draw in a non-specialist reader. Prehistory is a gift to the poet in that it can offer the mysterious, poignant detail as well as an intriguing archeological backdrop; it can present us with belief systems and artistic perspectives that are profoundly other to those recognized by contemporary culture.... There are vivid sensory details throughout, and often the poems themselves take on an element of liturgy... Vivid, evocative poetry engaging with ancient concepts of the sacred, and a rich prehistorical resource in its own right... This especially is strong poetry, offering startling insight borne of careful observation."
> – Sarah Law, *Amethyst Review*

"While museum artefacts do feature in poems, this isn't a collection set behind distancing glass. There are cave paintings – as they're being painted. Similarly, customs and traditions, gods and goddesses, burial sites and bog bodies aren't just described and dated; they're brought back to life on the page.... The poems generally are fueled by the flames of storytelling, with violent truths set alongside more positive elements of life.... Reading these poems isn't simply an act of second-hand witnessing, it's an act of experiencing. Yes, this is 'show not tell' in action, and also in keeping with contemporary emphasis on experience, given the seeming ephemerality or fast-changing pace of much of modern life (and prehistoric life in a different way).... Poetic care and crafting is evident in many ways throughout the collection.... I could examine and explore each poem in similar almost forensic, archaeological tagging detail and still return to find new aspects to awe me. Reading from poem to poem, page by page, through the whole collection in order also brings added links and threads between poems and re-appearances that create extra connections. There's lots to admire exploring the collection in this way, but it's also a pleasure to dip into *Bone Antler Stone* and read more randomly, feeling the lines and enjoying the images and emotions evoked.... For me, *Bone Antler Stone* isn't just a beautifully crafted, fascinating and addictive collection, it's also a timely reminder that past history is never just the past's."
> – S.A. Leavesley, *Riggwelter*

"[*Bone Antler Stone*] is an act of powerful sympathetic imagination that forges a connection between lost cultures and our own and that reminds us of our commonality as a species.... The poems themselves are mostly short, unrhymed, and as sturdily built as their subject matter. The tone is reverent and full of awe for the people, their artifacts, and the landscape itself.... throughout the book, there is

# ☙S4N Books

email: s4nbooks@outlook.com
author's website: www.wordandsilence.com

for Jenny and Evie

# ACKNOWLEDGEMENTS

*Albatross*: Migrations at the End of the Ice Age, Ring of Brodgar 2
*Amethyst Journal:* Sanctuaries, Esus with an Axe, Sucellus: The Wine God
*The Basil O'Flaherty*: Chauvet, Lascaux, Altamira
*The Big Windows Review*: The Seeress of Vix
*Crannóg*: Cauldron & Drink
*Cumberland River Review*: Oleneostrovskii Mogilnik Cemetery, Skateholm Cemetery
*The High Window*: Star Carr, Fire Houses, Pytheas in the Shetlands, The Wanderer (Flight to Orkney), Walking Birsay to Swannay, The Wanderer II (Flight from Orkney)
*Isacoustic*: The Brough of Birsay, St. Magnus Cathedral
*The Journal* (Wales): Long Barrows, Tormarton Ditch, To the Air
*Londongrip*: The Amesbury Archer
*Orbis*: New Families Arrive in Britain, Bronze Offerings in the Water
*Poethead*: Horses on Orkney, Skara Brae, Bone Antler Stone (Museum Pieces), Cuween Chambered Cairn, Song to Sequana, Song to Nehalennia, Looking for Nerthus
*Underfoot Poetry*: Last Meal, Haraldskaer Woman, Tollund Man, Kayhausen Boy, Damendorf Man, Grauballe Man, Lindow Man

a marked awareness of art's magic, strangeness, and immortality. Many of the people in the poems live (and die) as outsider artists within their cultures: the "hobble-headed," lame-footed smith in "Song to the Smith"; "The Seeress of Vix," with her "crooked look" and "knobbled walk"; and, among the "Bog Bodies," the Haraldskaer Woman ("They didn't dare to cut my hair / and I was thrown in alive under their envy"), the Kayhausen Boy ("But my bog dreams amid all that dead matter / were to me a song I will never leave"), and the Grauballe Man ("perhaps special, perhaps a source of shame / perhaps feared and gifted in my defect"), to name a few. Fittingly, in the book's final poem, "The Wanderer II (Flight from Orkney)," the poet, using Pytheas as his mouthpiece, envisions his own work as a continuation of art's regenerative power."
      – Tom Zimmerman, *The Big Windows Review*


"Tim Miller's poetry captures not just meaningful responses to encounters with the rich archaeological record of prehistoric Europe but also a deep understanding of the complex character of each find. His poetic insight brings each site to life and illuminates the dark and misty past in a way that archaeological reports cannot do on their own. From Stone Age landscapes and burials to Iron Age bog bodies, *Bone Antler Stone* evokes not only the mystery but also the humanity of the ancient world."
      – Peter Bogucki, Princeton University, and editor of *Ancient Europe, 8000 BC – AD 1000: Encyclopedia of the Barbarian World*


"Tim Miller's collection kindles a fire that we have forgotten; a fire that flickers on cave walls and builds a bridge between humankind and the pulse of the wild world beating beneath it. The poems are full to the brim with life, reimagining and rebirthing the lost years our own prehistory, dug from the earth like lost truths. An endlessly fascinating and beautifully written collection."
      – Wendy Pratt, author of *Gifts the Mole Gave Me*


"Another eye, another hand. Views on that other country that is the past vary widely. Tim Miller's evocative words touch many places in the past of Europe and call out to each of us regarding the uniqueness and importance of time and place. His thoughts offer a charm and intimacy with that past that I found enchanting."
      – T. Douglas Price, Emeritus Weinstein Professor of European Prehistory, University of Wisconsin-Madison, and author of *Europe Before Rome*

1
4
5
8
12
13
14
15
18
19
20
21
22
23
27
28
31
32

# LANDSCAPES
# & RITUALS

# FIRE HOUSES

All the old stories have their fire houses:
hostels, banqueting halls, stopping places,
some leading to the Otherworld,
some made of iron, and all of them
set afire, mansions made into ovens,
severed heads begging a drink of water.

I thought I saw this, driving home at dusk:
there was an old house set back off the road
and surrounded by the summer night's heat,
but what I took for flames was a thicket
backlit by mere electric light sprawling
from the TV, the kitchen, the bedrooms.

We do not know the note of invasion,
we don't believe in any Otherworld.
Where is there any great liminal space,
some resting place found on the borderland
where we might meet with every difference,
with true refreshment, or awful violence?

# CHAUVET, LASCAUX, ALTAMIRA

Now we come to paint with light and fire.
There is no violence on the walls, no pursuit or danger,
there are no landscapes, only waves of scraped and smoothed stone
    covered in intended color,
there are no hunted animals here, only the ones that fill us with
    reverence, bestiaries of awe and galleries of envy and
    appreciation,
bodies of strength and warmth depicted in their mating perfection,
    in the midst of their multiplying,
put on the walls with scaffold and ladder, paint tubes of hollowed
    bone or stem, animal hair brushes with the color still loaded,
    smokeless bone-marrow lamps and bear kneecaps filled like a
    bucket with pigment, with dye and daubs and splatters of stain
    and tincture,
the flicker of fire and shadow giving them movement, these animals
    who mean more than food and who are so important we carve
    and incise and draw and paint and put them high up,
some early underworld or merely a different heaven in the dark,
the caves always close to spring and river, so much of spring and
    pregnancy,
so much flowing and identification.


★★★


He beats the stalactite with an old bone
and from it finds an old song
with the flightier sound of a bird bone flute,
and to this I add my lamp and light it:
the ibex scraped on its bottom begins to warm
and the fuel of burning juniper
is the aroma of something other than myself.
And to this light I mix my colors with cave water,
I mix my colors with blood and vegetable oil –
and from the sweat of the stones and the heat of my light
an animal appears beneath my hands,
all surrounded by juniper green and unforgettable song.

***

The rolling, muscular, liquid walls,
rippled and erupting or hollowed,
all covered in bison and bear and reindeer,
in lion and rhino and horse and ibex,
bodies with no earth line as if in flight, rising out of the rock,
blurred legs of ash smudged by a passing hand
or a horse's head outlined forever into the soft white wall
as an afterthought, with the butt-end of a torch.

***

There is cave darkness without torchlight,
cave dim and silence, cave drip and echo,
but also fireblack from the charcoal hearth
dark as any dark from the well-fed flames
whose glow smells of pine
and whose light illuminates the chaos of animals.
Or how the ash is gathered for paint or pigment
and mixed to make red or left to blacken bone or flint or wood
to draw and scrawl and incise on the wall,
using the color of nothing to create everything.

***

Now the bear is the one who understands us –
and perhaps the bear was us, an older form
of human in how it stands on its legs,
some long ancestor preferring to sleep
for a season over any of our toil,
desiring the direct mystery of life
over our chosen mystery of mind.
No bear painted us, but we painted them,
no bear thought to prop up or set our skulls
on slabs or in niches or on ledges,
but this is what we did for them, in deep

veneration of their nerve and endurance.

★★★

A bison made by his hands, white hands dipped in red
and palms slapped on cold rock again and again,
smacked hands turned or righted or angled
and his exhausted step back to see
the animal made only of red palms and rock,
red like bison's blood, stone vitality,
his awe at a heartbeat behind the wall,
and his hands red as a midwife's.

★★★

Did the bears who tore at this wall to sharpen their claws,
did the bears who did this know of the bison
whose head would take shape from their scraping,
and do the bison we make in our heads
know how the bears help to make them,
the bear and the bison all bits of each other
and all of them in our minds,
until splashed on the wall with understanding?
Who put the impulse of making in my hands,
and who keeps us all under such watch?
Who is it that knows before me
what I and the bear and the bison will do?

*France and Spain, 35,000 – 12,000 BC*

# THE VILLAGE OF DOLNÍ VĚSTONICE

Come to stay at Dolní Věstonice,
where the floors are level and the walls of mammoth bone.
At night we have the fire and the bird-bone flute
and in our kilns we bake clay into shapes:
there's our mammoth that we love for food and clothing

and the very framework of our huts, a shape
we cannot escape and wouldn't want to;
and there is our woman and all that she does,
feeding breasts and bearing hips but also
her silent dialogue with land and moon

and all that swims out of their shared rhythms.
And these are our dead, dusted with ocher,
red for the grave and with necklaces
of fox teeth or ivory. They were loved.
And this is the larger fire where we gather

less for warmth than for oneness and light,
and the words of that one woman who wields
a mammoth shoulder and knows the Otherworld.
Though that fire is only lit in the dark,
by the light of shared words such clarity comes.

Czech Republic, 25,000 BC

# MIGRATIONS AT THE END OF THE ICE AGE

I like to think about it this way: that the
ice sheets of ancient Europe, rather than
melting and making a run to the north

simply because the weather got warmer,
instead retreated, were sought out and stalked,
harried and run down by animals, plants

and human tribes living off the new:
new forests, new seas, new islands, and new
places to settle, hunt or be hunted,

to die and be buried, ornamented
with the bone, stone and shell of this landscape,
their bellies full of water lily, pear,

salmon and horse, pig and seal and tubers,
the sky blue along with birch, oak and beech.
That's how I like to imagine the scene

from my own perch, some twelve thousand years on –
that the continents of covering ice
retreated from the hunt for new meaning,

every branch and drop and living thing made
to signify something more than itself,
up to the roasting scent of hazelnuts.

*10,000 BC*

# THE VILLAGE OF GÖNNERSDORF

They returned every winter to find things
mostly as they had left them: the slate floors
needed cleaning so the animals engraved

there stood out again in the dust of their feet.
Their huts needed more horse hide, though only
a few, not the full forty from when

they were first built. Carved tablets and figures,
thought lost, reappeared in last year's debris,
including a dancing scene they all loved.

Of the engraved animals, the same weren't
eaten, just as the creatures of the kitchen
were not carved. Which is not to say the hunt

wasn't holy: just watch them chase the horse,
the fox, the reindeer; just see how they spy
the geese in flight, and smile before firing.

*Germany, 9500 BC*

# STAR CARR

Beneath an assembly of birch and aspen
they settle the red deer, dead, on the ground.
His meat is mindfully removed, salted, and stored,
the rest of him slipped with dread and respect

into the good lake, with all the others.
Such deer crowd their bellies like nothing else,
and so crowd their minds and crown their heads, too:
skull cap removed and some bone scraped away,

skull cap perforated and a strap pulled through
to fit the head of a human being
antlered, weighed down, overwhelmed and aware.
And wearing that helmet, that other head,

did they commune there out on the water,
did they tremble on the platform made there,
and made with more care than their living space,
this door to all the deer that had fed them,

the deep lake and the submerged hunt magnified?

*England, 8500 BC*

# NEW FAMILIES ARRIVE IN BRITAIN

You would have watched them, weary at how they
all kept coming, and their courage to
give the tide their lot: cattle and tribe and plant,

family and farm filling a flotilla
of skin-wrapped ships, sheep and seed and children –
and all worse than war. They didn't need to win

but would, by insinuation and influence,
with some so sure of themselves they sailed on
for Cornwall or the Celtic Sea, skirting

the world's edge on another wrinkled wave –
pig and pottery, prayer and all that's precious
always changing by the reach and the march

over ocean and over again
of those risking removal and ruin
to weather life with those who never would.

*5000 BC*

# FIRE HOUSES II

Why would they do this to their houses
every other generation or so,
why would they gather the soul of a home –
pottery, the potter's wheel and the loom,
furniture and their fireplaces and

floors of laid wood covered in clay –
and bring more fuel, all to set it on fire?
Why when no enemy came with malice
did the whole community come as if
saying farewell to some dying neighbor –
why were houses treated almost as friends,

or as history before writing,
as exemplary as any story
of how the long past is recognized
and repeated overtop the ashes
where a new house with the same solemnity goes up?

*Southeastern Europe, 4000-3200 BC*

# NEWGRANGE

There would be no Newgrange without the sun,
no need without this ultimate ancestor,
no mound, no chambered passage and vaulted roof,
no carvings of circles and spirals and arcs
without this original ring, this coil
dug into the earth at the end of each day,
down into the ground where the dead are
but into the air every new morning –
the dead there too, on the trail of the sun always.

There would be no Newgrange without the Boyne,
the river and its reused pebbles or those
of the Wicklow, Mourne and Cooley Mountains
and a dozen places many miles distant,
beach and riverbed now walled interior,
a contribution from every direction
for this crown in the landscape, this turfed cap
dressed in a belt of sparkling quartz,
mirroring the sun and the size of a mountain.

*Ireland, 3200 BC*

# SONG TO THE SMITH

Hobble-headed, odd, and with a lame foot,
weird man – the weirdest – talking to nobody
but the fire's colorful heart, how it
dances and from its flames the stones of our
forebears are distended and beaten and poured,
stone the enduring sign of our ancestors,
stone the rough jagged bones of earth
suddenly smooth and luminous from his hands –
the solitary smith, the borderland smith,
the smith both dangerous and jeopardized,
honestly feared but then mocked for his impairment –
a lameness or a lag or a lazy eye –
concerned with the transformation we seek,
concerned with ground beauty, sun beauty, with
the voice of the dead in the metal's jarring clang –
but there's an equal trembling at such talent,
the attitude given to gods obeyed but not loved,
shamans and smiths two birds from the same nest,
the same unreliable nest and world
that requires their haunted gifts at all,
fear and hope a fusion in their fire
that their eyes and hands dance with and renew,
within them too much of death, too much of life.

# THE SEERESS OF VIX

Let my crooked look fall on you in life
and you'll be free of infirmity and pain
and our people will know the far future.
I may wander the earth with a knobbled walk
and this hard, twisted face I turn at you,
and while no man will spread my waddling legs
I already know how you'll bury me:
a thousand liters of wine in one krater
of bronze, a frieze of chariots and horses
on its rim and a gorgon gazing out
from each handle. I will be laid on a
wagon and adorned with Greek and Etruscan
treasure, with amber and diorite and iron,
with brooches and beads and rings and a torque
of gold round my neck fashioned at the ends
into the paws of a lion, and topped
with two tiny winged horses in ascent.
Not bad for a woman no one will love
and just right for a woman you can't ignore.

*France, 480 BC*

# SANCTUARIES

At some point the landscape was not enough,
or it was so necessary that we
were prompted to respond with our own hands:

boundary of stream and pool, frame of mountain
and forest, horizon of lake and plain.
And so, in a place to see it all best,

dig a ditch to enclose to widen out, with
post and wall and a roof over the central pit,
offerings as much to the underground

as to the wide sky and the deep valley.
Hang old weapons from the entrance, from the walls,
shields of rotting wood and leather, and swords

all broken and rusted, bent and dismantled –
even the embalmed heads of enemies,
and even the heads of offered cattle

become corroded skulls up in the corner.
What we erected had to rhyme with the land,
even though our clutter of offerings

and objects could never match the simplest
grove or lakeside, plateau or hollow or
the wordless, most unassembled spread of oak.

But we did our best with gold offerings
and the feast, with wine drunk and ritually spilled,
with every tribal action preceded

by some gift and question about the land,
about another war or more travel.
What we made by ourselves was a reminder

of our own bewilderment and ignorance
but also of the clues left us, the love,
the seasons and their mighty moods, the land

and its inclinations, the animals
and their whims and tempers and emotions.
Knowledge makes none of this any easier,

but meaning is meaning for being hard.

## THE SEAFARER

If not the fair wind, follow the fulmar:
at sunset they start for land, so seek them
and watch which shore their winds wind them to;
read the tides, recognizing their awareness,
but give in and go when the mother wave guides you,
the surge that swells with strength beyond the tide;
there are clouds too that only cleave to hard ground
and are marked well before the mainland is glimpsed;
but it's best to take your boat out at night,
to be steered the surest course by the stars,
to look and look and know those lamps
with as much warmth as any woman.
Fervor for the sea will finally free you from it.

# GODS & GODDESSES

## I. Esus with an Axe

As if he were winter itself
Esus goes at the willow tree,
goes to prune it back for a time,

promising a spring without blades.
And as if they were winter itself,
the egrets in the willow tree

consider how the cold must come,
consider where all souls must go,
and surrender the willow to fly.

And as if it were winter itself
the marsh beside the willow tree
cools and freezes and hides beneath ice,

beneath the cracking axe of Esus,
beneath the iron sun, iron clouds,
beside the low willow in winter.

## II. Sucellus: The Wine God

Every now and then, why not, give your time
to the drunk old man – the hammer he holds
struck winter out of the earth after all,
and gave us the grapes that got him all groggy,
the barrel overflowing and the jar
overturned, the amphorae running over.
He's not the most graceful god, not in spring,
but remember that his hammer is thunder,
that his hammer is the reliable wheel
and his body is covered in the serious
signs that the dark of deep winter were made for –
so join him while his hammer is on the ground
and while, stumbling, he gives a smile over at you.

## III. Song to Sequana

Source of the Seine, shrine and woman of the spring,
sanctuary to water's sudden appearance,
doorway to underground and Otherworld,
place to abide and feel close to the dead,
close to some culmination of the landscape
 – elsewhere a grove, elsewhere a rock, elsewhere
a single venerable tree, and here a spring –
draped lady in your boat, diadem on your head,
I bring a bronze body for my brother
I bring a wooden leg for my neighbor
I bring a stone head for my own ailment
so that by such illustrations you might
make the bodies of your pilgrims whole again.

*Burgundy, France, 100 BC*

Later, the Romans would love this horse goddess
and she would get the affection of the

hard-bitten legions, but there were
those in Burgundy and before who had her

in their houses, modest shrines of rapt feeling
for the one with corn and grapes and apples,

pine cones and pots of honey and of mead,
the one whose lap was loaded with bread and fruit,

or with a dog beside to lead the dead
into the Underworld. Her jangling keys

unlocked the stable and the afterlife,
plentiful mother riding side-saddle

or sitting at the thermal shrine to heal,
the meaning of cornucopia and countryside.

V. Looking for Nerthus



The priest senses a new weight in the wagon
and it's driven by boat to the mainland
and wheeled with rejoicing from place to place:

the pulling cows are feted and a new
festival for the goddess is founded,
food and thanks for the draped wagon, and all

weapons of war are hidden from her presence.
When she's had her fill of adoration
she's returned to her island and her lake

where she's washed among familiar confines
of grove and temple and shore, where she's bathed
along with wagon and hangings and wheels.

The image of a woman washed with lake
water and carried like the chariot
ferries the sun, or like the buried wagons

do the dead, bronze sun and horse and wheels:
the mystery of grove, lake and island,
since the slaves who bathed her are drowned there

for their knowing but necessary touch,
for the brilliant but dire revelation
that with everything they give, the gods are hard.

## VI. Song to Nehalennia

Lady, here are offerings for all those
whose business has to do with ships,
the ones from here to Albion and back
and the prow you always lean upon;

Lady, here are offerings for all those
whose business is with the worked earth,
the ones with herbs and flowers
and all the fruits piled upon your lap;

Lady, here are offerings for all those
who have ceased with commerce and died,
our sons in the sea and our fathers in the ground
and the Otherworld's dog always at your side;

Lady, here are fresh loaves from all those
that have desired your altar and temple and shrine,
the ones who follow your miles to the water
theirs and our mothers the long background of you.

*Netherlands, AD 200*

# FIRE HOUSES III: NAVAN FORT

For us there are only fire festivals:
a holy day is a day for heat
and what you call Navan was a livid flame.

On a hill in use for four thousand years,
where rings of timber and a surrounding ditch
somehow always seemed to find a way there,

we built our own roundhouse, four rings spiraling
in to a great pillar of oak, great eye
and great sun and great hub of the huge wheel.

But we filled that fiery house with stones
and burnt it and covered it over with earth,
a stone apiece for each one of our dead

and for them all now a mound in the landscape,
and for us all another entrance
into the Otherworld, where the setting sun

and all the gods can lift that heavy veil
to let us glimpse the host and their feasting,
and the smoke from that fertile, central flame.

*Ireland, 95 BC*

# THE SUN SETS INTO THE SEA

The sun sets into the sea with a hiss
and rises with the sound of a driven wheel,
the creak of speaking stone, metal and wood.

The sun sets into the sea to simmer
and rises with the sound of stretched leather
and the song of the horse's chain and bit.

The sun sets into the sea and is doused
and rises with the sound of reborn flame
rolling into another red morning.

The sun sets into the sea, and the sun
disappears down into extinguished light,
a golden disk diving to a dark blue.

But the sun rises as the night retreats
and rises like some cart out on the road
setting to the old labor of daylight,

a wounded wheel and an exhausted gear
chipped and scarred and with a battered hub
like an old mad father afraid to die.

But he always dies when winter comes and
sets colorless into the sea, grey sun
into the iron waves, the sound of sinking.

# BURIALS

# RED LADY OF PAVILAND

There was no North Sea then,
no Celtic Sea, only
land or ice from Calais
to Ireland, and his

cave now on the coast was
then seventy miles inland,
and for all that time
his bones were still dusted

with ocher, his necklace
still of periwinkle
along with carved bits of
ivory, antler and

bone. Dead in his twenties,
he devoured nearby
mammoth and the far flung
fish, either nomadic

in life or respected
in death to be shouldered
so far for burial,
only later boxed up

and taken to Oxford.
And how was it, thirty
millennia mostly
with the surf so nearby,

his relics still a call and
response with the sea,
the reverent spiral
of reddened bones and panorama?

*Wales, 31,000 BC*

# OLENEOSTROVSKII MOGILNIK CEMETERY

For them, the water and
the deep meant Underworld,
and so an island in
Lake Onega summed it up:

every spring or autumn
some new boat and body
accompanied by others
and by the drum, by swans

passing or the adored
waterbird – the one who
fashioned home everywhere,
land and air and the deep –

to the island on the rim.
Buried amid them were
pendants, necklaces, and
headdresses dreamt up from

moose incisors, bear tusks
and the teeth of beaver;
there were daggers of bone
and knives of slate, there were

harpoons and fish hooks and
antlers carved into the
likenesses of moose or snake
or an actual human face,

graves covered in ocher
and sealed by sand and a
covering of stone.
For a few centuries maybe

this is how it went for

five hundred of their dead, all
but the shamans facing east,
shamans west to where the

Underworld opens, shamans
like waterbird and bear,
shamans like moose and deer,
shamans of their three-tiered

world and their central world tree,
travelling that pole from
upper sky to middle ground
to Underworld, everything

linked from teeth to drum, from
swan to dagger and to
every bear, up the pole and
down, stars to scattered ocher.

*Russia, 6400–6000 BC*

# SKATEHOLM CEMETERY

Fill their bellies with fish
when death makes its approach

and our feast will be the same,
throwing bones and remnants

in the filling grave, their
bellies and our bodies

lavished with fish for life
or death. Whether man or woman,

give them tools or ornaments,
axes or animal-tooth belts,

and dress them in the rattled clothes
of sewn-in bones from the wild.

Dust their bodies red with
ocher, and give them the

crowned knives of the red deer –
give them some antlers for

underground, or their old dog.
Burn the platform over

the grave and mix earth and
ashes with all the bones,

all fuel and food and waste –
and remember the good death,

the well-observed dying.

*Sweden, 6200 – 4500 BC*

# AERØ BOAT BURIAL

Walk the handful of stones
out from the shore to the
shallow sea and the boat

is there, hemmed in by driven
spikes, trunk of a lime tree
hollowed out for him:

young man of twenty-five,
axe scar on his skull long
since healed, and dead of some

subsequent encounter.
For the afterlife he's
surrounded by the antlers

of the red and roe deer,
mementos and prophecies
of hunts old and hunts to come.

The rest of his boat is
a litter of mattocks
and flint slices, the sea

about him a bestiary of
otter bones and swan relics,
his body wrapped finally

– circles and layers of trees –
in a blanket of bark
still cleaving to him

upon discovery.

Denmark, 4790 BC

# LONG BARROWS

Forty or so people,
a few generations,
bones gathered and mingled,
laid in just after death
with their bodies stripped of flesh
or collected after
decades, the brittle and
the new integrated,
long collected or lately mourned,
neighbors bundled in dust
and identities lost
in some under-earth
roofed with timber and walled in stone
and wrapped over in grass,
green waves of long old life,
humps of them in the landscape,
small rises like murmurs.


# TO THE AIR

Not burial at all
but instead a great freeing,
flesh handed over to the
birds and elements,
dead lives widely scattered
and confined to no single ground.

Or the hunger of fire,
earth gods dusted with ashes
and sky gods smudged with our smoke,
the wide circle covered
and all of us everywhere.

# AJVIDE GIRL

She was twenty years old
and the garment she wore

is gone except for a fringe
of teeth: seal teeth, fox teeth,

and the teeth of a dog.
The hedgehog covered her:

its spiked skin capped her head,
and around her neck there hung

some five clattering jaws
she kept close, in a bag.

And at twenty, already
middle-aged, did she have

some love who thrilled to hear
the rattle of her skirt

as she slowly came near,
or the fall of her cap

to finger her young hair?

*Gotland, 3000 BC*

# THE AMESBURY ARCHER

Grown up amid the Alps
he crossed the continent

and sailed the Channel
to die near Stonehenge.

One kneecap was blown out
and he lived long with an

abscess in his jaw, but
he was buried with knives

and arrowheads, boars' tusks
and with the earliest gold

of England wound into
his hair. And among some pots

were the knapping tools and
the small anvil of a smith.

Revered and regarded
he died old at forty,

pain in his leg and jaw,
but within sight of the great stones.

*England, 2300 BC*

# TORMARTON DITCH

Roadside burial is all,
not even five abrupt
funerals, just tossed in
for covering over.
Two of them marred, pelvis
speared, the broken tips still
embedded, skull broken
open and spine transfixed
with bronze, some small skirmish
without ceremony
concluded with blood and
a quick unloading.

*England, 1500 BC*

# THE EGTVED GIRL

In the hollowed-out tree
they buried her, sixteen,
in a grave long waterlogged

that kept her clothes preserved.
Set down toward the dawn sun
and wrapped in oxhide, her

skeleton now is soil,
only her brain and nails
recovered in the cup of oak.

A miniskirt of string
lay strewn across her thighs,
her bare waist capped by a

belt disc, bronze, of carved spirals.
At her feet: a bucket
of birch filled with honey beer

beside a bundle of
cremated bones (a child,
not her own), both of them

strewn with yarrow petals,
white for a burial
in summer, closed trunk

in a closed barrow and
burial mound: in soil
closer to bog, to peat,

the warm, wet skin of earth.


*Denmark, 1370 BC*

# MAGDALENENBERG BURIAL MOUND

More than three hundred feet in circumference
and rising almost thirty off the ground,
a great round spiraling swell in the land,
a great green eye, a great wheel of earth

at whose hub far down is a barrow of
stones surrounding a room planked in oak:
some great man's body. And radiating out
all around him are a hundred more graves,

two or three generations of power
before it passed on to another
like some wind mistaken for eternity.
But for those few dozen years there was that hill

spiked with grave-markers and centered on some hero,
surrounding his life like constellations,
men and women become moon and stars
orbiting something other than the earth.

*Germany, 600 BC*

# CLEMENCY BURIAL MOUND

For the afterlife, see how well-fed I was:
ten amphorae overflowing with wine

(seventy gallons each), four pigs for the fire,
and a room under the earth for company.

For the afterlife, see how long they came:
around my mound are the remains of their feasts,

pig and wine, bones and the sacred fire,
their song and dance to me on the other side,

their words and adoration and reverence
unfurling the veil of timber and grass.

Luxembourg, 70 BC

# BOG BODIES

I. Last Meal

During a time of feasting and boasting and meat,
their stomachs are a bestiary only of grain,
bellies a mush with the barely digested
gruel of barley and rye and buttercup,
goosefoot and hawksbeard, linseed and clover
and knotweed, with spelt and yarrow all a last
twist or bit of weight above the waist,
a feeling of tough fullness near midwinter,
a last meal before being dragged away.


II. Haraldskaer Woman

My bones lasted down there, as did my skin
and my insides – but so did the stakes
that were hammered down to hold me in,
so did the weight of more branches belted
across my chest, and the same for a pile
of pointless clothes, since I was thrown in naked.
My hands were clean too, my body pristine
and even plump from a healthy fifty years.
They didn't dare to cut my hair
and I was thrown in alive under their envy,
since the hunger I never had would not
ward off the starvation they feared: their limbs
would still be thin come the ravening winter,
and another spring of unforgiving hunger.

*Denmark, 450 BC*

In the impossible photos it seems
you must really be cast in bronze
or carved with meticulously haunted care
by some Iron Age sculptor as expert
in the creases of your discovery sheet
as the vividness of your femur
beneath a two-thousand year-old cloak.
Naked except for this girdle and cap
 – and the rope used to hang you, still around
your neck and still with its imprint there –
you died horribly but are beautiful,
sleeping face and pointed cap and perfect feet,
a peat cutter's slash dug into your back
but preserved as none of your captors are –
though what a price for immortality.

*Denmark, 400 BC*

IV. Kayhausen Boy

I was already wicked in the legs,
that's what they all said when they saw me walk,
and that was why they gave apples to me
the last gift of sweet juice gleaming on my chin
before all the stabbing began. And why
bother I don't know, but they bound my worthless
feet after I was already dead, and
they bound my hands behind my back to the
binding already around my neck, as if
the bog might restore all my sinful limbs
and in that case that I might come for them.
But my bog dreams amid all that dead matter
were to me a song I will never leave.
Drink me some bog water and suck the leaves
down in the damp, down here in the dark
amid the muffled measure of a thousand hearts.

Germany, 350 BC


V. Damendorf Man

Damendorf Man is a flattened stone
Damendorf Man is a sheet of unused iron
Damendorf Man is a mulch of wet leaves
Damendorf Man is a line of blown ash
scattered in the shape of a crushed body,
limbs and skin and bones deflated under peat
like whole endless centuries of exhale
finally consummated in some museum case.

Germany, 300 BC

If I could I would have opened my eyes
that April spring day to see everyone
staring at my head no longer submerged;
it was very like the last crowd I did see
before they brought me naked here
and sliced me good from ear to ear.
You'll wonder why and look at my clean hands
that never worked the ground I was given to;
or the pain in my back that made me deformed –
perhaps special, perhaps a source of shame,
perhaps feared and gifted in my defect.
Perhaps they gave me to the gods because
in their bitterness and envy they knew
I was closer than anyone to them.
And if I could only see my picture now
you know I'd say they were right – what a head
flattened by centuries beneath the peat,
what an ugly body caved in or bulging
and displayed all twisted just as you found me,
knotted and gnarled into anything but sleep.
But don't you come to see my nakedness,
and haven't I been so preserved that my
fingerprints are as vivid as any
of your criminals? Isn't that reverence?

*Denmark, 290 BC*

VII. Lindow Man

The remains of my back are like laid tar
wrinkled and ribbed by my sudden spinal column.
My last meal was a loaf of bad barley
sprinkled with the hard magic of mistletoe.
Old at thirty my body ached enough,
and so why put me on my knees this way,
why strangle and kick me and slit my throat,
why crack the skull of one already in pain,
why the overkill, why three or four deaths
when one way left me lifeless enough?
What was it you saw in me which required
a body beyond limp to still be hanged,
what ghosts did already dead bones break
when I was tossed face-down in the moss?

*England, 58 BC*

# ARTEFACTS

# FEMALE FIGURINES



*for Evie*

Hum the words with me and you might understand:
mammoth ivory, hematite, limestone,
black jet, soapstone, antler and fired clay –
all of these become our bodies because
our bodies are the place of becoming.
They would not emphasize our hips and breasts
or underline the low triangled cleft,
and would not know to rhyme the bison horn
with the horned moon and our monthly flesh
without the genius our nine months gives them
in our seething, essential, swelling dark.
Feast and wear and build with bone, skin and sinew,
but by taking the time to make us
in the only way they can approximate –
hand-held bodies mostly handless, mostly
faceless, mostly propped up for gazing –
they make a simple bottomless mystery
of our bodies and the earth, the round year,
the rounded belly and the circled life.
Since they will never acquiesce to ours
they will worship strength and others like them
and will build to forget that they aren't it.
But sing the words with me and you might understand:
Lespugue, Laussel, Hohle Fels and Willendorf,
Brassempouy,  Dolní Věstonice
and Gönnersdorf – we've always been here.

# AXES

They would rather row out to Rathlin Island,
they would rather quarry the difficult

mountain over any easier spot
that happened to house the same stone. Demand

made the axes better, as did the withdrawn,
the journeyed-to, the arduous and removed.

Meaning over the merely efficient,
axes polished beyond the cutting blade,

beauty balanced with use, the whole consort
a dance of place, motive and exertion.

*Northern Ireland, 4000 BC*

# THE NEBRA SKY DISK

Five pounds of green-blue bronze in your hands:
disk of Cornish gold and Carpathian gold,
disk of Cornish tin and Austrian copper,

inlaid sun and crescent moon and seven
Pleiades between, in the bronze sky.
More stars scattered and the horizon right there

in two gold arcs on the outer curves
indicating the summer and winter
solstice in old Anhalt, old light and new,

gold as the sun and other stars
while beneath them all a golden boat
in its ascent – in our ascent – upwards

to a sense of the heavens, all in a
small disk, portable, for flight or silence,
for private reverie or public remark,

a stone circle or temple for one's pocket,
early science and old religion meeting
around this rim of bronze, in these strips of gold.

*Germany, 1600 BC*

# THE ULUBURUN SHIPWRECK

The cedar ship sank off the coast of Turkey
with pottery from Cyprus and jewelry
from Egypt and Mesopotamia,
with Baltic amber and African ivory,
with ingots and eggshells and colored glass and
a bronze goddess with gold-covered head and hands,
with sickles and axes and awls and a
handful of weights in the shape of a calf
or a sphinx, a duck or a frog, with
figs and almonds and cumin, with fish hooks
and a writing board perhaps to tally
up the whole – but the Mediterranean
swallowed the cargo down into the blue
on its way to Greece from Syria
and sank with someone's expected riches,
its crew drowned amid fishing gear and tools
wondering how much their bones would bring beside
electrum and turtle shells and scarabs,
their limbs flailing in protest as they plunged
while their shipment calmly complied to sink,
indifferent to surface light or to deep dark,
indifferent to highest shelf or to sea floor,
a storage jar of glass beads battered
by blind hands beating the underwater.

*Turkey, 1300 BC*

# BRONZE OFFERINGS IN THE WATER

Chant the name of Flag Fen if you like
but there are thousands of others all through
the Isles in the running rivers of Thames and Trent,
Shannon and Bann, and in many a still lake
and bog: huge hoards of bronze – weapons, vessels,
scraps and ingots or useless socket axes
soft and made in the thousands just to drown –
all offered to satisfy the waters
for some seven hundred years. At Flag Fen
a causeway of oak spikes and laid trunks led them
out over the water where the veil was thin –
to do what? To give the gods the metal
that was theirs, to ritually destroy wealth
in declaration of another, deeper
reality? Centuries of awe and fear
over this frantic feeding of the water:
bronze for the gods, bronze for the dead, bronze for
something other than their rich but hard life
where the landscape speaks but with no certainty?

*Britain and Ireland, 1300 – 600 BC*

# THE HAZEL ROADWAY

The only way to wander over the bogs
was with rods of hazel laid in a row,
the wingspan of wide trees put at one's feet,
branch by trunk over bog and impossible
landscape – and their swallowing squelch, should
one fall in for good. Nearby and later
entire seasons were spent dropping
alder and elm, yew and ash and endless oak,
layers of wood and rudimentary nails
laid over the bogs and all they augured
in their haunted impassibility.
Perhaps superstition fled with those roads,
or maybe they just bit at the ankles;
but in time the bogs drank all that wood
and preserved them there for us to find,
suggesting the benefit of the devoured.

*Ireland, 1000 – 150 BC*

# CAULDRON AND DRINK

They love their honey and they love the vine,
the wine and beer they engender with fire
and the altered world each takes them to.

They name their vessels like newborns, they name
their goblets and flagons and mixing bowls
and give titles to their cauldrons, those cornucopias

of bronze or clay or silver, a few or
a few hundred gallons deep for meaningful
intoxication and the huge feast,

faces beaten into the metal sheets
polished with running honey and mead and wine:
the gorgon or the boar or the winged deer

or the antlered god, legs crossed, the animal
master with serpent in hand and surrounded
by canine and feline and stag – and so

take a long drink and go for some outsized
strength, go for some feat of appetite and bragging:
drown your faces in grapes, drench your faces in gold.

# A SONG TO STONE

The hardened, quiet persistence of stone,
the longevity of our graves beneath them,
not permanent but very nearly so.
Our people should be stone, our families:
the seasons are stone, their circling endurance,
some slab in the landscape always there.
Love is stone, the gods are stone, stable,
the ground is stone in its always giving,
the rivers and the seas are stone, ceaseless.

But then, the most durable anything splits,
or the ground betrays us to starvation
and all the waters rise and overwhelm.
The gods can ignore us and the seasons tilt
and the oldest friends give way to frenzy
and violence, stone put to slaughter's use.
Yet none of these are so unlikely as failed stone:
instead, deepest veins in all directions,
exemplar of stillness and tenacity.

# SONG OF TREES

Canoe of lime with a paddle of ash,
fish trap of alder and fish spear of thorn,

bow of yew beside arrows of willow,
a fire from boxwood or laurel or oak

and oak also for building, with the rest
precisely chosen pine, linden, elder

or otherwise, all memorized texture
and give, strength and spring and pliability,

a lifetime's love of transfiguration,
the undying shuffle of shape and purpose.


# THE BATTERSEA SHIELD

Three circles stand out from the upright shield,
the shield thirty-three tall inches of bronze,
three rings in ceaseless relief filled as they
are with further scrolls and spirals and waves,
the rings within rings inlaid with colored glass
all a symmetry so lovingly shaped
it was never meant for any warrior
but instead for the Thames it was given to,
wealth and imagination better spent
on the gods of tendril and curlicue
and all the hidden faces suddenly
staring out from every mirrored curve,
eyes of glass and lashes of bronze
as fluid and flowing as the swallowing river.

*England, 200 BC*

# THE PAINTED STAGS OF CLERMONT-FERRAND

Glorious stag alive on the side of
a painted pot, impossible antlers proud
as they emerge like flowers from the head,

touching an equally unlikely tail
that flourishes up a back and over a
swerving torso more plant than animal –

or just more human than natural,
humor and elation and revelry
in the familiar made improbable,

in the already beautiful further
exalted with limbs of leaf and torso of stalk
all filled in with a smiling flourish of mind.

*France, 120 BC*

# ORKNEY

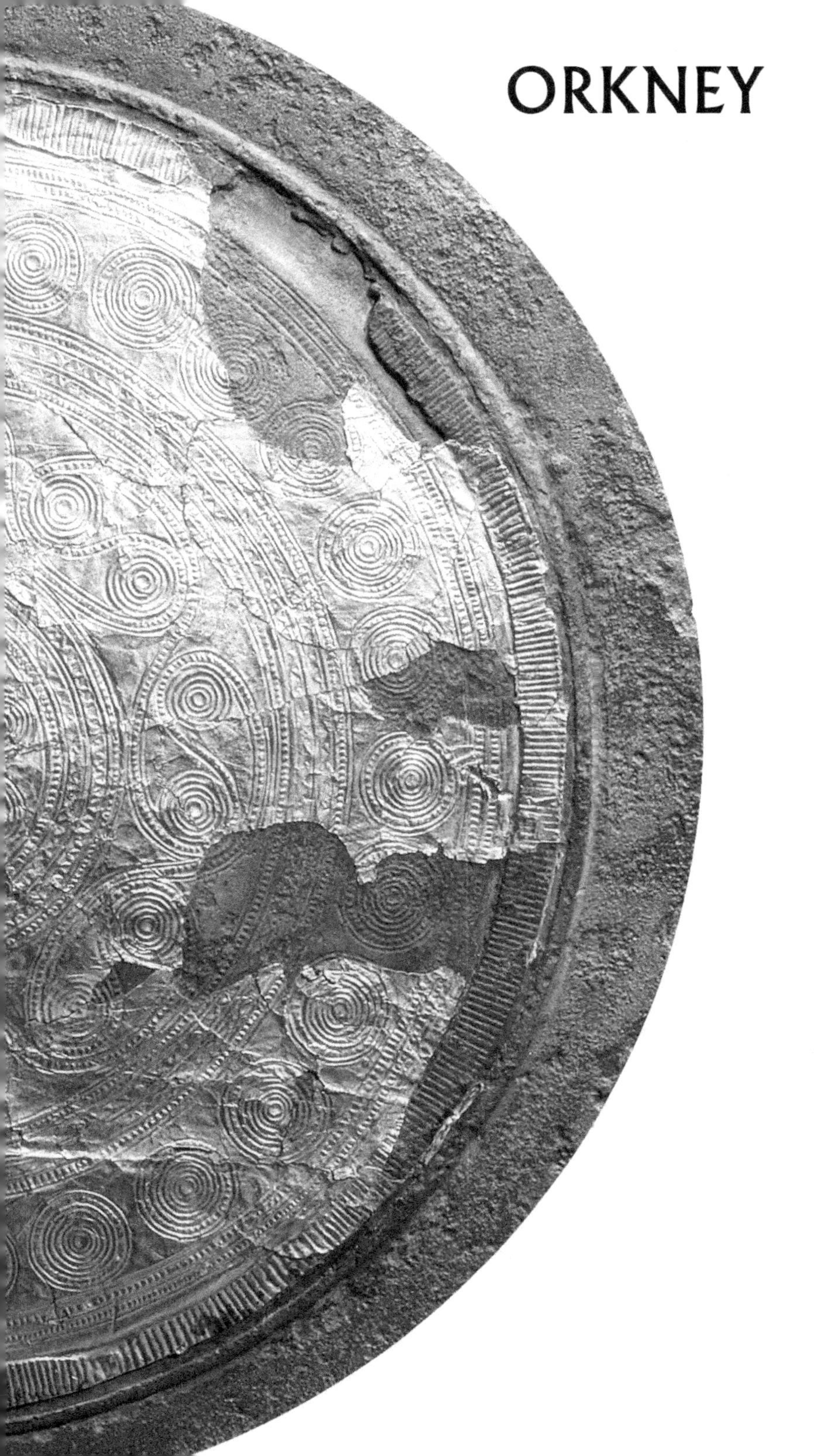

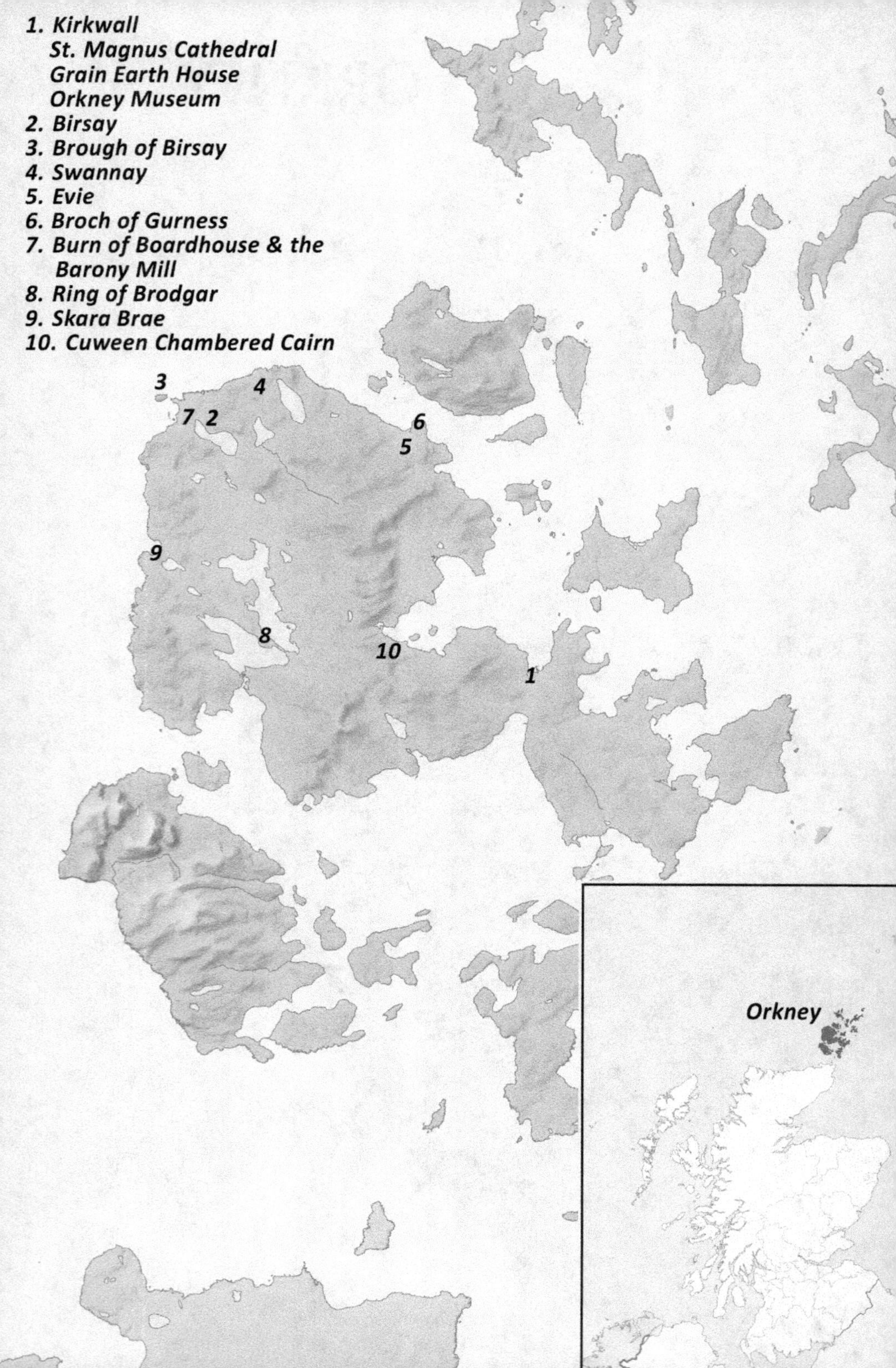

1. Kirkwall
St. Magnus Cathedral
Grain Earth House
Orkney Museum
2. Birsay
3. Brough of Birsay
4. Swannay
5. Evie
6. Broch of Gurness
7. Burn of Boardhouse & the
Barony Mill
8. Ring of Brodgar
9. Skara Brae
10. Cuween Chambered Cairn
3
4
7 2
6
5
9
8
10
1
Orkney

# PYTHEAS IN THE SHETLANDS

I imagine him in energetic
middle-age: young enough to be stupid,
seasoned enough to make it from Marseilles

and wise enough to want it at all, to
circle Britain from the tin mines of Cornwall
to the Irish Sea and the cold islands north.

An ancient Greek who never saw Athens
but who may have walked much of Albion
amid people and tongues already passed

into myth and exaggeration. But
he saw them sigh at the rain, saw them
quiet and real and lauding the seasons

in a thousand confidential gestures,
and in the Shetlands may have heard travelers
like himself – pilgrims worn by the hard sea

and the long ache of lonely navigation –
rise to grumble about further islands,
further north, further east, further west – and ice.

*325 BC*

# THE WANDERER (FLIGHT TO ORKNEY)

I met up with Pytheas there, on the plane,
the one heard from a hundred years after Herodotus
who turned Greek tradition into truth:
all the tentative talk of tin islands,

of mines and a mother source of amber –
Pytheas was the pilot who proved it,
from ancient France to the Faroes
through the threshold of the north to Thule,

and now next to me, so near
but still measuring and marking out the meaning
of the stars and the sea and the shafts deep
down through the dread earth delving for the veins,

his haggard head a mournful horde
of names and numbers and of navigation,
of what the world was and how it went,
those huge seasons spent hugging Albion's shore.

And seeing my slim book about him
he smiled somehow to see his world reshaped,
but as we descended he dissolved and died away
into a ninth and another wave, in the North Sea.

# KIRKWALL AIRPORT

Runes on the airport roof
spell Kirkwall
in an alphabet of branches,
and the boulders
lining the path to the bus-stop
(which anywhere else
would have been a bit of landscaping)
here seemed immovable
– or unmoved out of reverence:
some huge family
who had huddled up one winter
a thousand years ago
and never woke to warmth again.

# WALKING BIRSAY TO SWANNAY

I woke in Birsay and stumbled from the bus,
found a small shop with cereal and milk
and with these juggled between my arms and
with my laptop and some books on my back
I walked the three miles to Swannay along
the winding, windy road to our cottage.
While I'd already been up for a day
and only wanted to sleep for another
that flat curving road will never leave me,
two hours of long shadows and waning day
and clouds crawling as slow as me, always with
another stop and backward look at the
road receding, while the stubborn North Sea
seemed to stay where it was, always at hand,
the Brough of Birsay like a huge slim rock
skipped into the ocean centuries ago
by the flicked wrist of some bored god or giant:
and for those exhausted walking hours
that tidal island was my monument:
dipping away as the road rose, or how
it would slide to the left or right with the
curve of the blacktop and my controlling feet.
But mostly the fields were empty, mostly
those minutes were my own, the farmhouses
or cottages or homes of crumbled stone,
abandoned and jagged and roofless and
taken back by the yellow-green land –
mostly this was all, an all that was everything.
A few times I stepped into the high grass
to let the odd local drive by, and while
I had lost sight of the sea, near the end
the downward slopes of two hills met, and there
suddenly was a triangle of blue
and a northward glance that wouldn't hit land
until the ice and snow of the Arctic,
further seas and other islands made for

someone else's feet, if at all, since here
was the cottage I'd only seen photos of
back on another shore when this long walk
had only been a hint, only a desire,
and not the memory I cannot now shake.


# HORSES AND COWS ON ORKNEY

Horses curled in the flaming spiral of sleep,
the huge immensity of their bodies
belied by the blankets they wear, or the
tight scroll they twist themselves into on the ground,
an enormity suddenly made small
or at least passive, compact, the coiled braid
of body closer to tree or landscape,
the tilted, chiseled head nearer to stone
or to steel or something pulled from the fire,
some monument to just how this place works,
that you do not escape the wind, but dream in it.

★★★

The simple, curious staring of their eyes
and the enlightened calm either of their
drowsy, almost dreamy stroll or standstill,
completely at odds with their stunning size:
and in a landscape bereft of many
hills or trees, these great living bulks sufficed,
earth-born as these cows seemed to be, whether
the youngest, bold at its mother's udder,
or those old matriarchs sunning themselves
in the broken overcast, settled in
puddles of mud and tire tracks, fence-side.

# THE BROUGH OF BIRSAY

I.
Down the car park steps, down to the white beach,
down to the black clumps of sea-weed stuck up
through the sand like hair from a buried head –
heavy, flattened, green-brown leaves glistening
above some submerged and dreaming sand-filled head.

With mainland behind, Point of Snusan left,
scraggle of sea-road right and then straight North Sea
and the two of us caught between in the Sound
on the perpetually wet causeway,
the tide calm but always calmly coming.

Water shredded slightly, lightly rippled,
water terraced and layered by hard wind
and the slow assurance of certain tide,
whole forests of silken tangle swaying
to the pulse of algae, moss, and immersion.

Shelves of rock, tiered roadway into the sea
terminating not long after we'd left
into undertide, into simple surf,
simple sea-floor and abundance and deep,
and coated over with sheet and wave and song.

II.
There are only doors here, on the Brough,
the glazed windows are all in the grass,
bits of glass that once let you look out –

now only doors, now only entrances,
now only perpetual exposure,
no exit or escape from the wind,

my feet on gravel and sand silenced
by the unending complaint of air,

and the weakening cliff glancing down on

the great scarred shelf naked under sun,
looking like farmland carved and rutted
by rolling knives and great bladed wheels.

And I sat in one of those houses,
one of those houses without windows,
those lone houses now barely foundations:

I sat where there were no longer walls
and imagined opening the door
of morning to that cold, to that howl,

those scythes of white cloud over the blue,
the blue which rushes behind the wind
and steals the cliff-edge year to year,

Pictish houses already vanished
down the old throat and whirlpool of ruin,
the Norse houses we wandered nearly there –

and the devoured walls barely to my knees
all weathered but somehow unweary
and standing as any standing stones,

the strangeness of the Scottish flag there
incongruous to the sea-facing streets,
the smithy, the sauna, the paved hearth,

the warmth and steel of generations:
lives unlike ours, lives of basic green and
brown, slow but lacking relaxation

on the edge of hunger and safety,
this slope by the sea far from leisure
and far from want in its brutal need.

III.
Beside the Brough of Birsay white birds float
only a few feet from the cliff, to blue.
Wings wide, they hover as if on a string
until I see they're poised at the wind, strong,
as unable to advance as be defeated,
hanging still a hundred feet above the sea
until they turn, tilt into the current
and ride the air clear to the horizon.

IV.
Horrified of heights, I hung back
as you went to the world's wide edge,
to the bluff out back of the Brough,
over the cliff to the coiling current
that came to no country again until Canada –

and I stopped to hear some sniggering
and turned toward the lighthouse
to peer at Pytheas there, smiling
at the farce he found my fear to be,

saying if a height was hideous then all was horror,
all the world only wilting and worry,
and if I was afraid of a few hundred feet
I would never follow him as far as the Faroes,
could never continue as cold as he had been,
as hungry or hermetic as him
for the six days north to where the sun slept,
circling Iceland in and around the summer solstice –

and thus shamed, I shambled my way to your side
and looking over the lofty ledge
I saw down below bright humps in the blue,
seal at swim in the slow brutal sea.

# GRAIN EARTH HOUSE

I should go on my hands and knees to you,
phone-light or flash-light showing only circles
of grey-brown wall, damp with centuries,
the low tunnel a small curve leading to
a larger room, a tall rounded space
peopled by free-standing pillars – the past,
it seems, stationed there in the wettish dark,
eyes scooped out but mouth and voice still going.
Down here was where dairy and meat were stored
or grain from the earth saved again in the ground,
grain from the gods gathered and given back.
A root cellar quickly meant many things
when we turned the lights out in that chamber
and emerged changed a few minutes later
from the droning rattle of seed and source.

★★★


The unavoidable conclusion that
this place is a damp body, bones buried,
the slime and wet of thirsty, living stone,
something spinal, something central and polar.
no clock like this dripping, like this crouching
darkness that does not move, or need to.

*100 BC*

# BONE ANTLER STONE (ORKNEY MUSEUM)

The long bones of sheep spliced and made into hundreds of pins,
pulled from the animal and put to use, long buried but now
under glass,
The palmed cups of stone lamps, scooped out bowls for oil still
rimmed dark from prehistoric flame,
The unknown unfinished bulbous forms of worked stone, the shape
of a seated figure or a mountain, others random growths star-
shaped and hand-held, all of them a mystery,
Polished pieces of bone no bigger than a fingernail, polished
absentmindedly, grooved and smoothed by idle hands, precious
now as any tool, the working of some familiar mind,
Bones made into beads, bone bits the size of teeth perforated with
bone drills and strung through and worn, bone jewelry atop
garments of skin, all covering our own skin, our own bones,
Pottery fragments like serrated sleeves of dried and sand-buried
papyrus, pottery lips or jagged bases closer to dug up skull or
brain case, pottery the memory holder, or like broken-edged
ancient teeth welded to Neolithic gums,
A scattering of blackened pieces of pottery, earth-buried and soil
colored or charred, now laid out on a dazzling white shelf like
two dozen islands thrown to a glittering sea,
A bowl made from a whale's vertebrae: and what handles, what
depths, and how to eat when it's the container that fills you
with awe, a link from the sea monster's spine now in your lap,
steaming or cold, or some central cauldron for all to pull from –
or perhaps it's just expected, when one's neck or wrists are
hung with beads of whale teeth, its huge mouth now holding
the head high or just juggled in the hand like dice, or shaken
and left in the pocket for luck,
Carved antler points, worn from use or burning, hollowed and
perforated points and curves of bone for handles, for music, for
wearing, every animal a breathing storehouse of tools,
Stone cleavers, mattock heads of whale bone or rock, the stone
point of the prehistoric plough, or shovels smilingly made from
shoulder bones, since our shoulders would feel the ache: all
pulled from earth or peeled from skin to work the earth and

feed our own skin, this small glass case just some stone age
shed, sweat and muscles in their remains, spring and summer
work or salty from the sea, fragmented but content from the
long restful millennia in the ground.


## WALKING TO THE BROCH OF GURNESS

Another morning off the bus at Evie,
another straight road running off to vanishing,
hugged by fencepost, weeds and heather;
another morning with the slope
of another hill slanting towards us
for the hour or more it takes us to reach it, if ever;
another morning where the most distant land
is a dark blue, is nearly purple,
and close enough to the clouds as two coupled bodies;
all until the land fell away entirely into the coast,
into a sand filled with shells,
a land beaten by the scouring wind,
slow erosion the only fact here
alongside the green-blue water of Eynhallow Sound.

# THE RING OF BRODGAR

I.
I saw an old couple going slowly
to each stone and, with mangled hand or cane
they would palm a pitted section, slap it,
tap and nudge a test of its solidity,
or brace themselves, leaning in for rest.
They stopped at each stone to do this, sometimes
holding hands and seemingly guarded by
the faster flow of those who wound among them,
like wind around a corner. They were so small
and a few times looked up together at
the ten foot spike of sandstone they stood before
and seemed, crouched in their old age, not in awe
of something they'd come to see a few times
but a situation of stone they'd known
for all four thousand of its years, as if
those hands were still proud at having put it up.

II.
Our last afternoon of whirlwind and rock,
I would never say you emerged from the stones
but I did see you walk up a small rise,
I did see you casually stepping out of the
purple meadow, loch-born and flowing.
So, rather call the place sacred to thistle,
sacred to deep scars of entrenched heather;
rather refer to an avenue of
heather with some ring of stones added in;
because the stones are confined to their ring
of numbers: three-hundred forty-one feet
around, thirty or so of sixty stones left,
and the cratered depth of four thousand years.
But no numbers for blossom, no boundaries,
no pattern of crosshatching heather and
thistle, no plan in the two lochs, or the
panorama of slightly curved backs everywhere.

In every real way, the ring was placed here,
the ring of now pock-marked, planetary stone
weathered and stained green or yellow or white, or
spattered as if with ink out of the dark –
but the landscape was first, the stones only our
attempt at echo and veneration.

*2500 BC*


# THE BURN OF BOARDHOUSE AND THE BARONY

# MILL

The Burn of Boardhouse and the Barony Mill:
the words are beyond music and rhythm
or, they bring to them color and memory:
waves and waves of windy, sand-colored grain
bordered by grey barbed wire, high grass and
the bright shots of curled, uncoiling thistle.
And the rush of the burn to the sea, perpetual,
the haste and hum and somehow the languor
of water and its ways, past abandoned
outbuildings and the bustling mill, through fields
and beneath bridges and between backyards
to empty as ever into Birsay Bay.
There is no thrum like this running river,
the drawl and croon that still hasn't settled,
from the first archaic ears to stop and smile
to the afternoon we caught up to it.

# SKARA BRAE

Follow the alley of flagstones
to a slab door of wood or rock,
locked with a shaped bar of whalebone.
Inside, opposite the door, a
dresser stacked with pottery, wool,
beads of bone and shell, or pendants
of whale's teeth or the ivory tusks
of walrus and boar. The hearth is
central, the hearth is heat and light
and the cooking of all that's caught:
mutton and venison, gannet
and golden plover and lobster,
eel and salmon and mussel, cod
and crab and pork, gull and scallop.
Wild berries fill the belly too,
wild cherries, hazelnut, honey,
some form of fermented plant for beer,
or the richness of cows and goats.
Near the hearth a tank for fish bait
while beds and shelves curl around, all
surrounding the fire fueled by seaweed
beneath the rafters of whale ribs.
There's one building with no bedding
but still a hearth, always a hearth,
no metal yet but only stone,
only wood and bone: blades, mattocks,
whistles, fine points or polishers,
all undertaken so near the sea,
generations of food-waste, ash,
dung, bones, broken pottery, shells,
or a rope of crowberries – centuries
of families, layers of houses
stacked like rock atop each other,
farmers farming, hunters hunting,
a nameless North Sea and a still
nameless wind giving sound and flavor

to the landscape and the prized lives
that prompted those circles of stone,
that made an occasion of a
hill or loch, coast or height or isthmus.
Through the unknown, unremembered gate
we found the village and the bay
another excuse for green and blue,
five thousand years to our first world,
having flown far to propitiate
those who may have sailed from the south
to this true north, treeless and edged like a blade.

*3000 BC*

# CUWEEN CHAMBERED CAIRN

I should go on my hands and knees to you,
you farmers from five thousand years ago.
Even though your skulls are no longer here
or the small skulls of your two dozen dogs,

in retrospect I realize how wise
I was, dipping in and out of your dark
 – the familiar main chamber and three rooms –
to never pause in all my picture-taking,

to never stop and extinguish the light,
to have found your cairn at the end of the day,
so that we were tired and a bit rushed.
The terror of being in a tomb

would have overwhelmed me in the moment,
the seriousness of generations
which I only became aware of later:
like an ancient fireplace still smudged with smoke,

our shoulders were soiled from the gloom on your hands.

*3000 BC*

# ST. MAGNUS CATHEDRAL

In the sandstone walls of St. Magnus
are many migrations, many raids
and inroads and many an exodus,
many a generation spilling landless
out of the over-crowded north, farmless
and without wealth – or just caught up in youth
and ambition – with neighbors near and far
now the only ones to pay such debts.
Down from Denmark and Sweden and Norway
to Lindisfarne and Lisbon and into
the Mediterranean, or down
the eastern rivers to Constantinople,
down Volga and Dnieper to the Black Sea
either plundering monasteries or
hanged themselves and dangling from Moorish palm-trees
or sacking cities Abassid and Khazar,
everywhere their runes scratched into stone
or marble, befriending or destroying
Magyar or Bulgar or Muslim, Christian
east or Christian west, Saxon or Irish or Frank,
cities and villages and rivers all
still bearing the mark of their language and
the density and spread of occupation now
become habitation, winter camp to permanence,
centuries from seafaring to settlement,
from pagan to pragmatic convert
still with Thor's hammer and beside it a cross,
not fifty years separating the hanging
of hundreds of Frankish soldiers and the
plundering of Paris on Easter Sunday
to the establishment of Normandy
or the discovery and bare taming
of Iceland's impossible volcanic landscape,
ocean experts of cloud cover and bird flight
and the suggestion of more land far distant,
family and history everything to them

in later saga, biography and song.
     All this in the red-yellow walls of Magnus.
And of course the namesake's hallowed bones did not
do away with feud and betrayal,
but there is no need for the linguist or
archaeologist in a place never
buried and which has lived fully since its start:
the huge barrels of red sandstone pillars
blotched a seemingly fire-stained smoky brown
and still bearing the signatures of their making:
mason's marks of crows' feet, calipers or ploughs,
all the slightest lines but the farthest eyes
in the place, a hand brushed over these cuts sent
back to the time of the columns going up.
Or at waist level there are iron rings
bolted like brown eyes into the pillars,
a place for tethering horses unused
now except in imagining their feet
impatient on the floor and preferring
the bay or the roads or the stonewalled fields
or the standing stones as their own church of wind.
Or how leaning against every wall were
stones a few hundred rather than a thousand
years old, commemorating medieval dead
with hourglass and shovel and Latin,
with carved petals and the vault of heaven,
with a crown and clutching hand in the clouds,
with winged faces and the kneeling dead all
beside the words that they lived regarded
and died regretted, and are here today
with coat of arms and a kind of friendship
with death, stone poems and epitaphs to him
clustered about with oars and with bells
or grapevines climbing the columns or birds
carved atop a carved roof with another
hourglass and a bundle of fruit to
remember that refrain, Memento Mori,
remember death while you live so the living

might remember you when you are dead.
     And you remember how we put our hands
to each word or shape in thick relief,
curve of letter or flower like bodies,
like some braille into history from
Viking raids to World War Two, from lost at sea
to long voyages, Asia or Antarctica.
And so we said aloud the names we found:
John and Elspeth and Barbara and Brown,
and William and Evelyn and Arthur and Muir
all resurrected and taken home with us
and haunting us still, haggling and sleepless
until I finish these poems,
feeding as they do off our reverence.
     All of it and all of them were here
well before we came and would remain
whether we stayed or left or never returned,
yellow and red sandstone not something built
but something rough and dug up, something far north
or simply self-generated, rising
on its own to better view bay and city and sea.
And the stone heads looking down from the nave,
Green Man with face gorged on leaf and growth
and the Sheila-na-gigg grimacing and
rudely holding herself open or just giving
some mysterious invitation
we would never comprehend or exhaust.
Or hidden away high up in the clerestory
above the aisle of hour-glass graveslabs
there was a thin window of colored glass,
and our tour to the top was colored light:
unused stain glass leaning out of light boxes,
red stone made blue from the midday rose window
and the lamps looking down the long nave
from above, and the bulbs strung along the
narrow passageways veining throughout
and spinning up the spiral staircases:
along the spine and through every limb was

white light, grey light, afternoon overcast,
and out on the parapet was skyless light,
cloud light, sea light, bay light, and a hundred
feet above the churchyard grass, a bright dead light –
and the light of one afraid of heights, beaming
at such a height in the air, to be there with you.

# THE WANDERER II (FLIGHT FROM ORKNEY)

"That's the problem with airplanes," Pytheas said,
and he meant that there was no time to mourn:
we left the islands in literal flight,
and rather than the lingering, long look,
it was a daybreak dash, a quick death
from airport to plane to atmosphere.

By then our best words were garbled:
 *Stone and sound and sea*
 *Green glass, green grass, great Magnus*
 *Hearth and heather and weathered rock*
 *Burns and burials and Brough*
 *Horizon blue atop deep blue, and all that is beneath*
 *Old bones, old bodies, and all that is before*
 *The deep and the dark and the dead*
 *The shore and the shells and the shoulders of land*
 *The going to ground, the generations, and the gods*
 *The teeth of the tide and the teeth of deep time*

The price to pay for a place like that,
the price to pay for poems like these
are such scattershot, scarified syllables
born from a belief of having belonged,
but forced back among those who belong
so normally and naturally to anything
that our intensity is terrifying or just tiresome,
and so the dead and the damp doubleback
into just another of our silent, stone secrets.

So Pytheas proceeded in reply,
assuring me that for us, and for ours,
there was only the odd look, the old look, the awed look,
but rarely the real look of revelation,
or the consolation of having communicated.
And so the motive was to make meaning and memory
a kind of barrow burial in bloom
a garlanded grave underground

forged with turf and stone and fire and then forgotten,
until a propitious step or a sudden storm
blows open this book's binding
and lays each line out in the light again,
shells of syllables dotting the sand.
To be summoned by someone is always a surprise, he said,
and someday I would feel a spade on my skull,
someday I would stand up and start singing,
but until then I should love the loneliness and its lessons,
and he bade me to build it well, to bury it well, and wait.

# NOTE

Near the end of his *Kaddish*, Allen Ginsberg asks, "What have I left out?" A small book of poetry covering many thousands of years of history might ask the same question.

For one, the Norse and Celtic myths that originally pointed me towards the archaeology of ancient Europe will have to wait for their own book, something I hope to call *Northern Metamorphoses*. Also, it's strange that both the emergence of agriculture, as well as the warrior aspect of ancient Europe – the first immensely interesting to me, the second not at all – are nevertheless both absent here. And the same with so much else left to chance, choice, ignorance, or idiosyncrasy. It's interesting, for instance, that the name "Red Lady of Paviland" (p. 26) has stuck, even though the remains have since been determined to be that of a man. Peculiarity and tradition rule.

Poetry is something similar, a rare illumination amid huge darkness, some attempt at eloquence and stability amid the run-on of mostly forgotten speech and words. Every poem is a rescue operation, and so I feel lucky to have found and recovered even these. This is one reason each poem's presentation is something like a museum placard: starting from the title and date, anyone caught by a particular poem should have no problem finding more information.

For those who want to look beyond these poems, the set of books that got me into the subject was the massive *Ancient Europe, 8000 BC - AD 1000: Encyclopedia of the Barbarian World*, edited by Peter Bogucki and Pam J. Crabtree. I can also recommend anything by Barry Cunliffe and Miranda Green, especially the former's *Britain Begins* and *The Extraordinary Voyage of Pytheas the Greek*, and the latter's *Symbol & Image in Celtic Religious Art*.

For the bog body poems, of course they wouldn't exist without Seamus Heaney's poems in his collection *North*, and we both took so much from P. V. Glob's classic, *The Bog People: Iron Age Man Preserved*; but I've also gained even more from that book's successor, Wijnand van der Sanden's *Through Nature to Eternity: The Bog Bodies of Northwest Europe*.

Jean Louis Brunaux's *The Celtic Gauls: Gods, Rites and Sanctuaries*, and T. Douglas Price's *Europe Before Rome* (the latter probably the best general introduction to the period) are two wonderful books I came to late in the writing, as was Felix Müller's *Art of the Celts: 700 BC - AD 700*.

And while there is only one poem devoted to them, I would regret not mentioning the following books on the painted caves of France and Spain: *Lascaux: Movement, Space and Time*, by Norbert Aujoulat, *The Cave of Altamira*, edited by Pedro A. Saura Ramos, *Return to Chauvet*, by Jean Clottes, and *Becoming Human: Innovation in Prehistoric Material Culture*, edited by Colin Renfrew and Iain Morley.

Scholars of cave art, and archeologists of ancient Europe in general, will (I hope) forgive the impression some of the poems might offer: that is, that cave art over the course of twenty thousand years, or that the technological or spiritual lives of those in Europe for a few thousand years BC, can be thought of as some easy unbroken chain of tradition and continuity, all summarized by some grand theory. Creative, popular, and academic writers have all been guilty of romanticizing (or just trying to "solve") the unknowns of the past with huge sweeping explanations, and I hope I haven't done that too much here. At the end of the day these are poems, but I have tried not to sacrifice history to that end.

Special thanks needs to be given to David Cooke of The High Window Press, for taking this book in the first place, and for placing many of its poems in his journal of the same name; and to the poet Daniel Paul Marshall, whose comments on specific poems, and correspondence in general, were invaluable during the writing of this book. The historian and longtime friend Kim McQuaid also gave a late draft of the book a thorough reading and offered many suggestions, as well as enthusiasm. And while they've already been mentioned in the beginning of the book, my wife Jenny and my daughter Evie deserve the most thanks: it is the gift of breathing my daily life with them that birthed these poems most of all.

www.ingramcontent.com/pod-product-compliance
Lightning Source LLC
Chambersburg PA
CBHW070914160726
48004CB00003B/1370